Introduction ....

CU00407324

iii

The Complete Air Fryer Recipe Book

Easy and Delicious Air Fryer Recipes for Fast and Healthy Meals incl. Bonus: Keto Diet and Low Carb Recipes

[1st Edition]

Thomas P. Owens

What is an air fryer?

An air fryer is an electric appliance designed to produce similar results to a deep frying machine. However, unlike a regular deep fryer it uses only a small quantity of oil and hot air to fry food to a crisp crust. Although the air fryer only became popular recently, it has been around since the year 2010 when it was patented by the Philips Electronics Company.

An air fryer is quite similar to a countertop oven. The appliance has a fan which blows air around within its cooking chamber at a high speed and a heating element that heats the air. An air fryer can be used for cooking fried treats such as chicken, fries, veggies and so on. Just like a deep fryer, an air fryer has a perforated basket on which the food sits. This ensures optimum contact with the hot air.

How it works

As mentioned, an air fryer is a miniaturized version of the countertop convection oven. Unlike a deep fryer which requires the food to be submerged completely in a pool of hot oil, the combination of hot air and little oil gets the job done in an air fryer. Hence the name. The appliance operates on the principle of convection.

Typically, an air fryer has a heater and a fan. The fan blows air into the cooking chamber and this air is heated up around the lightly oiled food in the fryer basket. The fact that there isn't much space between the basket and the walls of the cooking chamber further intensifies the heat produced in the fryer. This makes the food crisp on the outside via a browning reaction and well-cooked on the inside. The result is a significantly healthier fried food (since less oil is used). However, it may lack the taste and consistency of traditionally deep-fried food since oil penetrates and adds flavor to the food.

Air Fryer Maintenance

First, it is important that you clean your air fryer right after using it. Of course, no one likes the extra work but it is something you will have to do to keep your air dryer in pristine working condition. The good news here, however, is the fact that air dryers are quite easy to clean. Since you are using very little oil you won't have to bother about scraping some greasy mess off the fryer. Also, since a lot of air fryers are dishwasher safe, cleaning them will be quite convenient as well.

For parts that cannot be cleaned in a dishwasher, here is a simple cleaning procedure you can use:

First, you will need the following items:

- Soft Microfiber or cotton cloths
- A sponge (non-abrasive)
- Dish soap
- Baking soda
- Soft toothbrush of bristle brush

1. First, switch off the unit and unplug it. You should leave it for about 30 minutes to allow the various parts you want to clean to cool off.

2. Using a damp cotton cloth, wipe the machine's exterior. You should use the non-abrasive sponge and some hot water to wipe the interior as well.

3. Next, you should clean the heating element using the non-abrasive sponge. You should turn the appliance upside down for easy access to the element.

4. Make a paste using water and baking soda and use this to scrub off any hard dried spots of food residue both within and outside

the appliance. You can scrub the unit first with the sponge then wipe it with the microfiber cloth

5. Usually, the basket and the pan can be easily cleaned in a dishwasher in most air fryer models. Ensure that your unit is dishwasher safe before loading it into the machine. However, if they are not, a simple scrub with the sponge should be enough. To remove stubborn residue, you can them in hot water for a while and scrub again with the non-abrasive sponge.

With all the parts cleaned, air dry them all or wipe with a clean dry cloth before you reassemble the unit.

Cleaning an air fryer-Important points to note

· To prevent your air fryer from getting too gunky, it is advisable that you grease it before you begin cooking. You can also put a piece of foil or parchment down in the fryer.

· You can clear bad odor in your air fryer by putting a half lemon or some lemon juice in it. Leave for 20 or 30 minutes. Clean then rinse the pan and basket.

· Avoid using metal utensils, hard scrubby sponges or steel wool to clean air fryer. Abrasive materials like this will scratch off the non-stick coating on the fryer.

· Do not submerge the entire fryer in water. Only parts that are dishwasher safe should be removed and cleaned in a dishwasher.

Additional maintenance tips

In addition to regular cleaning, here are some tips to keep in mind to avoid damaging your air dryer and prolong its life:

- Before each use, inspect the cords to ensure that it isn't damaged. Avoid plugging a damaged or frayed cord into an electrical outlet as this can be fatal. Inspect other components as well before each use and replace broken parts.
- Check and clean air fryer unit before each use.
- Place in an upright position on a level surface away from walls and other appliances before you begin cooking. Air fryers typically need about 4 inches of space above and behind them for proper venting of steam and hot air. Hence using them in an enclosed space is not recommended.

Tip 1: Preheating your air fryer ensures that your food is cooked evenly:

Although this isn't a rigid rule, preheating your air fryer can save you some cooking time and help your food cook more evenly. This makes sense since an air fryer operates on pretty much the same principle as a convection oven. Hence, it is recommended that you leave the fryer on for a few minutes before you add your food to the basket. Your food might still turn out delicious if you don't do this, but I recommend that you do.

Tip 2: Before you begin cooking, it is advisable that you grease your fryer basket.

Although fryer baskets typically have non-stick coatings, it is still advisable that you grease it before you begin cooking. This way nothing sticks to the basket. You can use oil that have very high smoking points like soybean or safflower oil for this.

Tip 3: You don't always need oil on your food

While you might have been told to add a little oil on your food to make them crisp, you don't have to do this for all food items. Food with some fat in them already such as ground beef, fatty cuts of meat or dark meat chicken do not need oil. Vegetables like potatoes or any battered seafood require oil for crisp cooking.

Tip 4: avoid using non-stick aerosol spray cans on your air fryer:

Aerosol spray cans are known to contain additives that may damage the coating on your air fryer basket. Hence it is advisable that you avoid them. You can go for alternatives like an oil mister or spray bottle and fill it with your oil instead.

Tip 5: Avoid overcrowding the basket:

Placing too much food into the air fryer basket at the same time isn't recommended. Your food might not crisp as well as it should. If you have a lot to fry you should simply purchase a bigger fryer or cook your food in small batches.

Tip 6: Shake the basket if you are cooking smaller food items

To ensure even cooking especially with small food items like french fries or chicken wings you open the air fryer and shake the basket every few minutes. You can use a pair of kitchen tongs for flipping larger items instead of shaking the basket.

Tip 7: Adding water to the drawer will prevent smoking when cooking fatty food

Food items with high fat content like bacon, burger or meatballs may prove difficult to cook in an air dryer since they tend to smoke as the fat heats up. One simple solution is to turn off the fryer and drain it off then resume cooking. Alternatively, putting a little amount of water in the drawer tray may also help as the water prevents fat smooking by regulating its temperature.

Tip 8: Spray with oil again halfway through cooking

This is particularly true for coated food items and less fatty meats. Spraying with oil halfway through the cooking will help you get the best crisp. Spray the dry spots on food coated with flour halfway through the frying for perfect crispiness.

Tip 9: small light items might get swept up in the fan

Air fryers use a powerful circulation of hot air to cook food. The powerful fan at the top of the unit can cause lightweight items to be swept up into the fan and this can be very dangerous. One common culprit is seasoning powders and spices. They tend to be blown around by the fan. A simple solution is to mix them with oil to be used for coating the food instead of putting them on directly

Tip 10: Turn down the temperature for some food

Some food items dry out very quickly if the heat on the air fryer is too high. While you might want your food to cook faster turning the heat down on some food items like brownies will make them cook a lot better thank cranking it to the highest heat.

Tip 11: The dripping in the drawer is useful

You can still use the melted fat in the pan for your cooking so don't throw it all away. It is typically filled with flavor can be used for making pan sauces, gravies, and other recipes.

Tip 12: You should clean up after each use

Let you air fryer cool down for some minutes and clean up the basket, the drawer and the rest of the appliance. Cooking with the fryer without prior cleaning might be quite annoying as you may notice smoke coming out of the machine due to a residual buildup of oil and grease.

Time: 40 minutes | Amount: 2 Servings

Ingredients:

- 1 Apple (medium) (or pear)
- Chopped walnuts(2 tbsp)
- Light melted margarine (1 1/2 teaspoon)
- Cinnamon (1/4 teaspoon.)
- Nutmeg (1/4 tsp.)
- Water (1/4 cup)

How to prepare:

1.	Preheat air fryer to 350º F or 180º C
2.	Halve the apple/pear. Around the middle area, spoon some of its flesh out
3.	Place apple or pear into your air fryer's frying pan or directly at the bottom of air fryer
4.	Mix the margarine, cinnamon nutmeg, walnuts and raisins inside a bowl
5.	Spoon the mixture into apple or pear halves
6.	Add water into pan
7.	Bake in air fryer for 20 minutes

Ingredients:

- 1 lbs/0.4 kg frozen bread dough (thawed)
- Melted and cooled butter (¼ cup)
- Brown sugar (¾ cup)
- Ground cinnamon (1½ tbsp)

For Cream Cheese Glaze

- Softened cream cheese (4 oz/ 113g)
- Softened butter (2 tbsp)
- Powdered sugar (about 1¼ tsp)
- Vanilla (½ tsp)

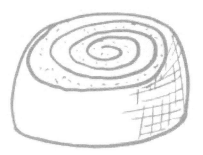

How to prepare:

1.	Allow bread and dough to come to room temperature on a counter.
2.	Roll the dough to form a 13 inch by 1 inch rectangle on a floured surface
3.	Position dough so that the 13 inch side of the rectangle is facing you then brush all over with melted butter. Leave a border of about 1-inch uncovered along the edges on the side of the dough away from your position.
4.	Mix cinnamon with the brown sugar in a bowl. Sprinkle mixture over buttered dough.
5.	Make a log with the dough by rolling it from the edge close to you. Ensure that you roll evenly and push out air pockets that may be trapped within. Press dough onto the roll on the uncovered edge to seal it.

6.	Cut the edge into 8 pieces (be careful not to flatten dough as you cut)
7.	Turn slices over placing them on their sides then cover with clean towel. Keep this for 2 hrs rise.
8.	To prepare glaze, put butter and cream cheese together into a small microwave-safe bowl. Soften mixture in microwave for about 30 second. Gradually add powdered sugar and stir. Add vanilla extract then whisk. Set aside the glaze.
9.	Preheat air fryer to 350° F/180° C.
10.	Transfer four rolls into air fryer basket. Cook for 5 about minutes. After 4 minutes, turn rolls over and air fry again. Repeat this for the second set of four rolls.
11.	Leave to coll for some minutes then glaze with large dollops of the cream cheese glaze. Allow some of the cream cheese glaze to drip slightly down the sides of rolls.

Time: 25 t0 35 minutes | Amount: 6 to 8 muffins

Ingredients:

- Cashew milk (or any diary or non-dairy milk based on your preferences) (1/4 cup)
- Eggs (2 large)
- Vanilla extract (1/2 tsp)
- Monkfruit (1 and half cups) (or any preferred sweetener)
- Baking powder (about 1 teaspoon.)
- Cinnamon (1/4 teaspoon)
- Fresh cranberries (1/2 cup)
- Salt (1/8 teaspoon)
- Chopped pecans (1/4 cups)

How to prepare:

1.	Add milk, vanilla extract and eggs into a blender jar and blend lightly for about 20 to 30 seconds
2.	Add almond flour, baking powder, salt and cinnamon then blend for another 30 to 45 seconds.
3.	Switch off blender and remove jar from base. Stir in the pecans and fresh cranberries into the blend. Add mixture to muffin cups
4.	Top each muffins with some of the fresh cranberries
5.	Place muffins in air fryer basket then bake for 15 minutes at 325º F/163º C
6.	Remove and allow to cool on wire rack
7.	You can drizzle muffins with maple glaze or melted white chocolate if desired

Ingredients:

- 2 pic crust (refrigerated)
- Cornstarch (1 tsp)
- Low sugar strawberry preserves (1/3 c)
- Philladelphia cream cheese (1 oz/ 26g) Reduced-fat
- Plain vanilla Greek yogurt non-fat (1/2 cup)
- Sugar sprinkles (1 tsp)
- Stevia (1 tsp)
- Cooking Spray

How to prepare:

1.	Lay pie crusts on a flat surface. With a pizza cutter or knife, cut the pie crusts into 6 rectangles (2 for each crust). Ensure each of them is fairly long and will fold over completely to close pop tart.
2.	Add cornstarch and preserves to a bowl then mix well
3.	To the upper area of the crusts add a table spoon from the preserves mix
4.	Fold each crust over to close pop tarts
5.	Create vertical and horizontal line imprints along the edges of the pop tarts with a fork
6.	Place pop tarts in air fryer then spray with cooking oil
7.	Air fry for 10 minutes at 375º F/190º C.
8.	Mix Greek yogurt, stevia &cream cheese to create frosting
9.	Allow tarts to cool before you remove from the air dryer to avoid breaking. Top each pop tart with some frosting then sprinkle some of the sugar sprinkles

Ingredients:

- All-purpose flour (11/4 cups)
- Baking powder (1/2 tsp)
- Sugar (1/3 cup)
- Salt (3/4 tsp)
- Baking soda (1/2 tsp)
- 1 egg
- Buttermilk (1/2 cup)
- Vanilla (1 tsp)
- Unsalted butter 2 tbsps + 1 tbps for brushing ((melted and cooled)

For the filling

- Strawberry or blueberry jelly (1/2 cup) no preserves

For the Glaze

- Powdered sugar (1/2 cup)
- Peanut butter (2 tbps)
- Milk (2 tbsps)
- Sea salt

How to prepare:

1.	Whisk the flour, along with sugar, salt, baking soda, and the baking powder in a bowl
2.	Mix your egg, buttermilk, vanilla and melted butter in a different bowl.
3.	In the bowl of dry ingredients make a well and pour in the wet mixture. Mix with a fork then stir mixture using a large spoon until well mixed
4.	Turn dough onto a floured surface. Work slightly until it comes together. Pat the dough to a thickness of about 3/4 inches.
5.	Cut out dough using a 3 1/2 inch cutter then brush with melted cutter. Cut out about 2 inch parchment paper to wrap each cut of dough. Place in an air dryer.
6.	Fry in an air dryer at 350º F or 180º C for 11 minutes. use a pastry bag or squeeze bottle to fill doughnuts with jelly.
7.	Whisk glaze ingredients then Drizzle over doughnuts.

Time: 25-35 minutes | Amount: 12 yields

Ingredients:

- Self rising flour (2 and half c)
- Monk Fruit (or any preferred sweetener) 1/2 cup
- Avocado oil (1/4 cu or any light oil)
- 2 eggs
- Blueberries(1 cup)
- Lemon zest (form one lemon)
- Lemon juice (from 1 lemon)
- Vanilla (1 tsp.)
- Brown sugar (for topping)

How to prepare:

1.	Mix self-rising flour with sugar in a small bowl. Set aside
2.	Mix cream, with lemon juice, eggs, oil and vanilla in a bowl
3.	To the mixture of liquid ingredients, add dry ingredients. Stir until it is fully blended. Stir in the blueberries
4.	Spoon batter into cupcake holders. On each muffin, sprinkle some brown sugar (about 1/2 tsp for each.
5.	Bake in air dry for about 10 minutes at 325º F/163º C until lightly browned or until is passes the toothpick test. Check at 6 minutes to ensure the muffins are not cooking too fast.
6.	Remove and leave for a while to cool.

Time: 15 minutes | Amount: 2 servings

Ingredients:

♦ Wholemeal Bread (4 slices)

♦ Eggs (2 large)

♦ Whole milk (1/4 cup)

♦ Brown sugar (about 1/4 cup)

♦ Nutmeg (a pinch)

♦ Honey (1 tbsp)

♦ Icing sugar (a pinch)

How to prepare:

1.	Chop whole meal bread into soldiers. You should get 4 soldiers from each slice of bread
2.	Place all ingredients except the icing sugar into a mixing bowl and combine thoroughly
3.	Dip each bread soldier into mixture until is is coated with it. Place these into air fryer.
4.	Turn on air fryer to 320º F/160º C for about 10 mins until bread becomes nice and crispy. Turn over the bread halfway through your cooking to ensure it is evenly cooked
5.	To be served with some fresh berries and a sprinkle of icing sugar

Time: 20 minutes | Amount: 2 servings

Ingredients:

- Egg white (1 cup)
- Skim milk (2 tbps)
- Sliced tomato (1/4 cup)
- Sliced mushrooms (1/ 4 cup)
- Chopped fresh chives (2 tbsp)
- Fresh black pepper

How to prepare:

1.	Preheat the air fryer at 320º F/160º C
2.	In a large sized bowl, mix all your ingredients
3.	Transfer mixture to the frying pan provided with your air fryer (or to the bottom of he fryer after removing accessories
4.	Back in fryer for about 15 mins till thoroughly cooked.

Time: 10 minutes | Amount: 4 toasts

Ingredients:

- Bread (4 slices)
- Milk (⅔ cup)
- Vanilla (⅔ cup)
- Cinnamon (1 tbsp)

How to prepare:

1.	Mix the eggs, milk, cinnamon and vanilla in a bowl. Beat till it combines fully.
2.	Dip each slice of bread in the mixture then shake to get excess off.
3.	Place wet bread slices into the prepared pan then place in your air fryer
4.	Bake in air fryer at 320° F/160° C for 3 minutes. Flip over. Continue to bake for 3 more minutes
5.	Remove from air fryer. Serve with maple syrup

Time: 30 minutes | Amount: 8 pieces

Ingredients:

- Finely grated potatoes (4 large)
- Corn flour about 2 tbsp
- Salt (added to taste)
- Pepper powder (added to taste)
- Garlic powder (1 tsp) optional
- Chilli flakes (2 tsp)
- Onion powder (optional) 1 tsp
- Vegetable oil (2 tsp)

How to prepare:

1.	Soak shredded potatoes in some cold water. Drain water after a short while. Repeat the draining process to get rid of excess starch
2.	1 one teaspoon of oil to non-stick pan. In it, saute potatoes for 4 minutes. Set this aside and leave to cool in a plate
3.	Add the corn flour, pepper, garlic and onion powder, & the chilli flakes into a bowl. Mix thoroughly. Spread this mixture over plate of potatoes and pat firmly with your fingers
4.	Keep Refrigerated for 20 minutes or more
5.	Preheat dryer to360° F or 180° C.
6.	Remove refrigerated potatoes and divide into smaller equal pieces with knife
7.	Place these pieces in the air fryer basket for about 15 minutes. Be sure to flip hash brown at the 6 minutes mark to ensure uniform frying
8.	Remove from air fryer. Serve hot with ketchup.

Time: 2 hours | Amount: 6 servings

Ingredients:

- Plain flour (450g/1lb)
- Butter (75g/2.6oz)
- Whole milk (277ml)
- Olive oil
- Coconut oil (1 tbsp)
- Yeast (5.5g/0.19 oz)
- Salt
- Pepper

How to prepare:

1.	Mix butter into flour until it is well combined.
2.	Warm milk and some oil in a pan (until they are lukewarm). Add yeast and the mixture of milk and oil into the bowl of flour and mix till a dough is formed
3.	Knead bread for 5 minutes, use a damp tea towel to cover the bowl of dough and set side in a hot place. leave for about an hour then repeat the kneading process for 30 minutes
4.	After though has proved, make it into bread roll shape.
5.	Make the dough into medium sized buns and place bread buns in a way that they tough each other in other to make the bread easy pull apart.
6.	Place bread rolls into airfryer and cook at 365oF/185oC for about 15 minutes

Time: 10 minutes | Amount: 4 slices

Ingredients:

- Ciabatta (4 slices)
- Salted butter (1 tbsp)
- Crushed garlic (3 cloves)
- Dried parsley (a few pinches)
- Grated Parmesan (freshly grated) 1/4 cup

How to prepare:

1.	Preheat air fryer to 180oC / 360oF.
2.	Place butter in a bowl, warm up in a microwave for about 10 seconds until softened.
3.	Mix in garlic, parsley and cheese into butter
4.	Spread butter onto the slices of ciabatta
5.	Arrange buttered slices in air fryer and air fry for 3-5 minutes. Check after 3 minutes to ensure it is properly cooked.

Ingredients:

♦ Multigrain bread or any similar bread (8 slices)

♦ Potatoes (2 large) boiled & mashed

♦ Grated or minced ginger (1 tsp)

♦ Coriander powder (1 tbsp)

♦ Chilli powder (to taste)

♦ Garam Masala (to taste)

♦ Cumin powder (1 tsp)

♦ Dry mango powder/ Amchur (1/2 tsp)

♦ Salt

♦ Water (1 large bowl)

♦ Cooking oil

How to prepare:

1.	In a large bowl, mix mashed potatoes with all your spices. Mix these throughly until it forms a smooth filling. Divide into 16 parts, make a ball with each and set aside.
2.	Place bread slices on chopping board. Cut them into small rectangles. You can cut out the sides if you think it is too thick.
3.	Pick half slice of bread and dip quickly in the bowl of water. Take out immediately squeeze between you palms to remove excess water
4.	Place stuffing ball prepared earlier on the soaked bread slice
5.	Wrap the soak slice round the stuffing. Wrap tightly until no stuffing shows outside
6.	Preheat air fryer at 390oF/185oC for 3 or 4 minutes.
7.	To each prepared bread, brush lightly with oil using a silicone brush to prevent bread from sticking to fryer basket (not compulsory)
8.	Spray the air fryer basket using cooking spray or oil then place prepared bread rolls in air fryer. Cook 6 to 8 at a once depending on how big your air fryer is.
9.	Cook for 15-18 minutes or till bread turns golden brown on all side. Turn the bread rolls after about 10 minutes of cooking.
10.	Serve hot with Green cilantro chutney and tomato ketchup.

Time:2 hours | Amount: 8-10 servings

Ingredients:

- Pizza dough
- Olive oil (1/8 cup) for baking sheet
- Chopped garlic cloves (2 to 3)
- Olive oil (1/2 cup)
- Red pepper flakes (1/4 tsp)
- Rosemary, basil or thyme (optional)

- Chopped parsley (1/2 cup)
- Chopped red peppers/ tomatoes (optional) (1/2 cup)
- Black and green olives (1/4 c ach) (halved) optional
- Pepper
- Salt

How to prepare:

1.	Preheat air fryer to 360oF/ 180oF and prepare a pan that fits into air fryer.
2.	Spread olive generously on a 11 x 15 inches baking sheet. Set this aside
3.	Remove risen dough from bowl and spread on prepare baking sheet. Punch dough with your fingertips to make some indentations. Set this aside. (punch again if dough rises after a while and dents disappear)
4.	Heat olive oil in a saucepan.Add the chopped garlic. Cook for some seconds. Add the red pepper flakes then leave on fire to simmer for 1 minute. Add in parsley and olives the some pepper and salt to taste. Allow the flavors to blend for about 5 minutes.
5.	Pour the oil mixture on the dough. Spread with a spatula to cover then brush more oil around dough edges if required
6.	Bake in air fryer for 12-15 minutes. (might be less if dough is thinner)

Ingredients:

- 2 (1/4-oz.) packaged Yeast
- maple syrup (2 tbsp.)
- 3 tbsp. warm water (110° to 115°)
- Softened butter
- silken tofu (1/2 cup)
- 4 large eggs
- 2 c. shredded, smoked gouda or smoked cheddar cheese
- 1 tsp. kosher salt
- Ground black pepper (1/2 tsp.)
- 5 c.King Arthur Unbleached Bread Flour, divided
- sweetened dried cranberries (1 cup)

How to prepare:

1.	In a small bowl, whisk yeast with maple syrup and water. Leave this mixture to foam a foam for about 10 minutes.
2.	Blend tofu with butter inside a mixer fitted with a paddle until mixture becomes light and fluffy. To this mixture, beat in eggs (one at a time) then stir in the cheese. Add yeast mixture, some salt and pepper. Also add 4 cups of flour and blend well using a dough hook.
3.	Mix in cranberries. Gradually add in the rest of your flour until it forms a soft dough.
4.	Knead dough for 8 minutes at low to medium speed until it reaches a smooth and elastic consistency. Transfer this dough to a prepared bowl. Leave for an hour (covered) until it rises to about double.
5.	Deflate dough and split into two portions. Shape each portion to form round loaves measuring about 6-7 inches. Place both loaves in two buttered round cake pans. Leave covered for another 45 minutes
6.	Preheat air fryer to 400oF/203oC. Make an X-shaped slash across the loaves (should be about 1/4 inches deep) place in fryer for about 20 minutes and cook until it turns golden brown. (target temperature of 200 degrees)
7.	Remove from the fryer. Turn out on the rack to cool

Time: 20 minutes | Amount: 4 Yields

Ingredients:

- 4 pork chops (boneless)
- Extra virgin oil (2 tbsp)
- Parmesan (freshly grated) 1/2 cup
- Kosher salt (1 teaspoon)
- Garlic powder (1 teaspoon)
- Paprika (1 teaspoon)
- Freshly ground pepper (1/2 teaspoon)
- Onion powder (1 teaspoon)

How to prepare:

1.	Pat pork chops with some paper towels until it is dry. Coat both sides with oil
2.	In a medium sized bowl, combine parmesan and the spices. Use this mixture to coat both sides of the pork chops
3.	Place chops in air fryer basket. Turn on the heat to about 375º F/190º C for about 9 minutes. Flip the pork chops when it is halfway done to ensure uniform cooking.
4.	Add the marinara sauce, some water, and pepper, and boil
5.	Turn down the heat. Leave to simmer for 5 minutes uncovered then add the tomatoes, olives, cheese and one tablespoon of basil

Time: 17 minutes | Amount: 1 serving

Ingredients:

- Ribeye or New York strip steal (1)
- Kosher salt (added to taste)
- Black pepper (added to taste)
- Garlic powder (added to taste)
- Paprika
- Butter

How to prepare:

1.	Leave meat to sit for some minutes at room temperature. Spray steak with some olive oil on both sides.
2.	Add kosher oil, garlic powder, paprika, and black pepper to season meat
3.	Preheat air fryer to 400º F or 204º C
4.	Place the steak in air fryer and allow to cook for 6 minutes, flip steak and leave for another 6 minutes
5.	Add butter as topping.

Time: 26 minutes | Amount:3 servings

Ingredients:

- 3 pork chops (6 oz./170g each) rinsed and patted dry
- Black pepper
- Salt (to taste)
- Garlic powder
- Smoked paprika
- Breadcrumbs (1/2 c)
- Egg (1 large)
- Cooking spray

How to prepare:

1.	Season the pork chops with some pepper, salt, garlic powder and smoked paprika
2.	Put breadcrumbs in a medium bowl
3.	Beat egg in another bowl.
4.	Dip each pork chop in egg then dredge in breadcrumbs to coat completely
5.	Spray the both sides of coated pork chops with cooking spray.
6.	Preheat oven to 380° F/ 190° C for about 4 minutes
7.	Place pork chops in air fryer. Cook for 8-13 minutes. Flip the chops after 6 minutes to ensure uniform cooking
8.	Cook until golden brown or until the internal temperature is about 160°F/72°C
9.	To be served warm

Time: 22 minutes | Amount: 4 servings

Ingredients:

- Cooking spray (any type of rub-on oil can work as well)
- 4 Boneless and skinless chicken breasts about (8ounces/226g)
- Black pepper (1/8 tsp)
- Dried oregano (1/2 teaspoon) (you can use thyme, parsley or any similar seasoning of choice instead)
- Salt (1/2 tsp)
- Garlic powder (1/2 tsp)

How to prepare:

1.	Mix the salt, oregano, garlic powder and pepper in a small bowl
2.	Spray cooking spray on the smooth side (presentation side) of each chicken breast.
3.	Sprinkle some seasoning on chicken breasts. Pat with your hand to make the seasoning stick
4.	Place the chicken breast in the air fryer with the seasoned side down. Then spray the other side as well and sprinkle the remaining seasoning on it.
5.	Cook at about 380° F/ 193°C for about 10 minutes. Then flip over and cook for another 8-12 minutes.
6.	Remove basket. Leave to to cool for about 5 minutes. This ensures that the juices redistribute making it juicer before you cut.

Time: 26 minutes | Amount: 4 servings

Ingredients:

- Ground beef (1 lbs/ 0.45kg)
- Salt (1 tsp)
- Garlic powder (1 tsp)
  Black pepper (1/4 tsp)
- Onion powder (1 tsp)
- Burger buns
- Worcestershire sauce (1 tsp)

How to prepare:

1.	Preheat air fryer to 360° F/ 183°C.
2.	Place raw ground beef in a bowl the add seasonings
3.	Mix everything with your hand or a fork then mold into a ball within the bowl
4.	Score the mixture into 4 sections by making a + sign then scoop out each section to form into a patty. Place these in the airfryer (ensure that each patty does not touch each other. (cook in batches if it is necessary)
5.	Cook for 6 minutes. Be sure to flip halfway through cooking..

Time: 2 hrs10 mins | Amount: 3 servings

Ingredients:

- Chicken pieces (with bone in and skin on) 2 lbs/ 0.9kg
- Buttermilk (2 cups)
- Hot sauce (1/2 c)
- Kosher salt (3 tsp)
- All-purpose flour (2 cups)
- Garlic powder (1 tsp)
- Ground pepper (1/2tsp) freshly ground.
- Onion powder (1 tsp)
- Oregano (1/2 tsp)
- Cayenne pepper (1/4 tsp)

How to prepare:

1.	Trim chicken to get rid of excess fat and place inside a large bowl
2.	In a medium bowl, mix buttermilk, hot sauce and 2 tsp of salt.Pour mixture over chicken. Ensure that all the pieces are coated.
3.	Cover, and keep refrigerated for at least 1 hour (you can leave overnight)
4.	In a pie dish or shallow bowl, mix flour and 1 tsp of salt and other seasonings.
5.	Remove chicken from butter milk mixture and place in the flour mixture. Turn until each piece is completely coated (work one piece at a time)
6.	Place the coated chicken pieces in air fryer. Ensure basket is not overcrowded. Cook at 400º F/ 204ºC for 20-25 minutes. Flip halfway through. Repeat the process for all the chicken pieces.

Time: 14 minutes | Amount: 3 yields

Ingredients:

- 1.5 lbs/ 0.68kg (Newyork or Ribeye steak) cutto 3/4 inch cubes
- Salt (1/4 tsp) + 1/4 tsp for asperagus
- Oil (1 tsp) + 1/2 tsp for Asparagus
- Black pepper (1/2 tsp) Freshly ground
- Dried garlic powder (1/2 tsp)
- Cayenne pepper (1/8 tsp)
- Onion powder (1/2 tsp)
- Montreal steak seasoning (1 tsp)
- Asparagus (1 lbs/ 0.45kg) with tough ends trimmed (or spear of zucchini)

How to prepare:

1.	Preheat air fryer to 400F/204C
2.	Trim steak to remove excess fat and cut them into cubes
3.	Add ingredients for the marinade (oil, salt, Montreal seasoning, garlic powder cayenne pepper and black pepper) into bowl. Toss steak with this ingredients . Massage the ingredient into the meat until it is evenly coated
4.	Spray air fryer basket. Spread prepared meat along the bottom of the basket
5.	Cook for 6 minutes
6.	Toss asparagus with oil and salt until it is evenly coated
7.	Once browned, toss the steak bites around then move to one side in the air fryer basket. Add asparagus and cook for about 3 more minutes
8.	Remove steak tips and asparagus and serve while hot.

Time: 4 h 50 minutes | Amount: 4 Yields

Ingredients:

- 1 lbs/0.45 kg beef sirloin steak (in small 1 inch cubes)
- 8 oz/226g button mushrooms (sliced)
- Worcestershire sauce (1/4 cup)
- Olive oil (1 tbsp)
- Parsley flakes (1 tsp)
- Paprika (1 tsp)
- Crushed Chile flakes (1tsp)

How to prepare:

1.	Combine the steak and mushrooms in a bowl. Add Worcestershire sauce, parsley, olive oil & Chile flakes to the bowl
2.	Cover and keep refrigerated for 4 hours or leave overnight
3.	Remove from the refrigerator about 30 minutes before you begin cooking
4.	Preheat air fryer to about 400F/204C)
5.	Drain marinade from steak mixture and discard. Place steak and mushrooms into air fryer basket
6.	Cook for 5 minutes. Toss and cook for 5 additional minutes
7.	Transfer to serving plates after 5 minutes.

Time: 2 hrs 25 mins | Amount: 2 servings

Ingredients:

- Rib-eye steaks (2) cut, (1/2 inch thick)
- Grill seasoning (4 tsp)
- Olive oil (1/4 cup)
- Reduced sodium soy sauce

How to prepare:

1.	In a large re-sealable bag, mix steaks, soy sauce, seasoning and olive oil. Leave for 2 hours or more to marinate
2.	Remove steak from the bag and drain off marinade
3.	Add a1 tsp of water to air fryer pan. This prevents smoking'
4.	Preheat your fryer to about 400oF or 200oC
5.	Cook steaks in air fryer for about 7 minutes. Turn steaks over and cook for additional 7 minutes till the steaks are medium rare. You can increase cook time to about 16 minutes for medium steak
6.	Remove steak and leave for 4 minutes then serve.

Time: 45 minutes | Amount: 4 servings

Ingredients:

- 1 lbs (0.45kg) lean ground beef
- 1 Lightly beaten egg
- Dry bread crumbs (3 tbsp)
- 1 Finely chopped onion (small)
- Salt (1 tsp)
- Freshly chopped thyme (1 tbsp)
- Ground black pepper
- 2 mushrooms (sliced thickly)
- Olive oil (as needed)

How to prepare:

1.	Preheat air fryer to about 400F/200C
2.	Mix the ground beef, bread crumbs, eggs, onions, sat, pepper and thyme in a large bowl. Knead till it is well mixed
3.	Transfer mixture to baking pan. Smooth the top
4.	Press the mushrooms into the top the coat with the olive oil
5.	Place pan in the air fryer basket and place in the air fryer
6.	Cook for about 25 minutes. Roast meatloaf until it is nicely browned
7.	Leave to rest for at least 10 minutes. Slice into wedges and serve.

Time: 15 minutes | Amount:3 to 4 servings

Ingredients:

- Tilapia (1 lb/0.45kg)
- Flour (1/2 cup)
- Panko crumbs (1 cup)
- Eggs (1 or 2)
- Chilli powder (1 tbsp)
- Lime juice (from one lime)
- Salt & pepper (added to taste)

How to prepare:

1.	On a wide plate, Mix salt and panko then add chilli powder and salt
2.	Scramble egg in a bowl. Put flour in another bowl
3.	Spray air fryer with some cooking spray
4.	Dip tilapia in fry flour, then in the egg. Press the tilapia in the Panko mixture until it is completely coated by it.
5.	Place coated tilapia in air fryer and spray with some cooking oil
6.	Cook in air fryer for about 8 minutes at 375oF or 190oC. Flip then cook for 8 more minutes until it is cooked through
7.	Remove tilapia from fryer and squeeze some lime juice over it.
8.	Can be served with pico de gallo, some lime wedges and avocado

Time: 25 minutes | Amount:2 servings

Ingredients:

- Fresh flounder fillets (2)
- egg (1, beaten)
- Breadcrumbs (1 1/2 c) (Whole wheat or any of your choice
- Salt and pepper (added to taste)

For Sandwich

- Sub(2 rolls)
- Iceberg lettuce
- Tomato (sliced)
- Optional-lemon wedges, coleslaw, pickle spears, fries and mayo.

How to prepare:

To prepare flounder	
1.	Dip each flounder fillet into egg. Coat this with bread crumbs, pressing the crumbs into fillet until it is thoroughly coated
2.	Air fry until cooked through for about 12 minutes
To prepare sandwich	
3.	Split sub rolls into two halves. Top these with tomato slices and lettuce
4.	Place flounder fillet on roll carefully
5.	Top this with tarter sauce or Mayo. Can also be served with wedges, fries, coleslaw or pickle spears if desired.

Time: 25 minutes | Amount:4 servings

Ingredients:

- Flounder fillets (4)
- Mushroom slices (4 oz/125g)- grind into smaller bits
- Breadcrumbs (1 tbsp)
- Green onion(2 tbsp)
- Lemon juice (1/2 lemon)
- Salt and pepper
- Mayo (1/3 cup)
- Lemon zest (from one lemon)
- Paprika (1/8 tsp)

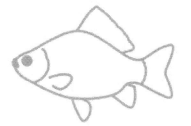

How to prepare:

1.	Mix mushroom, green onion, bread crumbs with lemon juice in a bowl
2.	In another bowl prepare a mixture of Mayo, paprika, lemon juice and lemon zest
3.	Season the flounder fillet as preferred. Place flat size of rhe fillet up then brush with mayo mixture.
4.	In each fillet spoon some of the mushroom mixture. Spread this evenly then roll each fillet similar to a jelly roll.
5.	Air fry without flipping for about 400oF or 204oC

Time: 10 minutes | Amount:2 servings

Ingredients:

- 2 Tilapia or white fish fillet (6oz/170g)
- Garlic powder (1/2 tsp)
- Lemon pepper seasoning (1/2 tsp)
- Onion powder (1/2 tsp) optional
- Black pepper
- Kosher salt
- Fresh parsely (chopped)
- Lemon wedges

How to prepare:

1.	Preheat air fryer for about 5 minutes at 360°F/180°C
2.	Rinse the fish fillets and pat dry then spray with cooking oil. Season the fillet with some onion or garlic powder on both sides. Add salt, lemon pepper and and black pepper to taste
3.	Lay the perforated baking paper in the air fryer. Spray this slightly with some oil to prevent fish from sticking
4.	Lay fish gently on the prepared paper. Next to it, add some lemon wedges
5.	Place in air fryer for 12 minutes
6.	Sprinkle fillet with chopped parsley
7.	Serve warm with some toasted lemon wedges.

Time: 30 minutes | Amount:4 servings

Ingredients:

- Cod (4 pieces) 1lbs/0.45kg each
- Sea salt
- All purpose flour (2 tbsp)
- 2 eggs
- Panko (1/2 cup)
- Onion powder (1 tsp)
- Fresh minced dill(1 tsp)

- Paprika (1/2 tsp)
- Dry mustard (1/2 tsp)
- Lemon zest (1/2 tsp)

For yogurt dip:

- Non-fat Greek yogurt (1/2 Cup)
- Fresh lemon juice (2 tsp)
- Fresh dill (1 tsp)
- Sea salt

How to prepare:

1.	Preheat air fryer to about 400 degrees F/205 degrees C and spray the mesh basket with some cooking oil
2.	Pat cod till it is dry the season with salt.
3.	In a large rimmed plate, pour flour. In another bowl, beat egg.
4.	Place panko and other ingredients into a large rimmed plate and stir until well mixed
5.	Coat each cod pieces with the flour, followed by the egg mixture. Place into the bowl of panko. Coat the fish with panko until it is evenly covered
6.	Place into air air fryer basket but do not stack to allow enough space between the pieces .
7.	Spray with cooking spray. Cook for 10 minutes then Flip over. Cook for an additional 10 minutes. Flip again and cook for about 2 minutes until underside is crisp again.
8.	Mix all the ingredients for the dip while the cod cooks.

Time: 25 minutes | Amount:4 servings

Ingredients:

- ◆ 2 medium potatoes (1 lb/0.45kg each)
- ◆ Olive oil (2 tbsp)
- ◆ Pepper (1/4 tsp)

To prepare fish

- ◆ All purpose flour
- ◆ Pepper (1/4 tsp)
- ◆ 1 egg
- ◆ Water (2 tsp)
- ◆ Crushed cornflakes (2/3 cups)
- ◆ Grated permesan cheese
- ◆ Salt (1/4 teaspoon)
- ◆ Haddock or cod fillet (1 lb/0.45kg)
- ◆ Tarter sauce (optional)

How to prepare:

1.	Preheat air fryer to about 400°F/205°C.
2.	Peel potatoes & cut them lengthwise. Each slice should be about 1/2 inches thick
3.	Toss potatoes with oil, pepper and salt.
4.	Place potatoes in air fryer basket (fry in batches if necessary) cook till tender for 5-10 minutes. Toss to redistribute. Cook till lightly browned & crispy. Remove fries and keep aside (keep warm)
5.	Mix flour & pepper in shallow bowl. Whisk egg and water in a separate bowl.
6.	Toss cornflakes with cayenne and cheese in another bowl
7.	Sprinkle your fish with some salt, then dip into it into flour mixture to fully coat. Shake off any excess flour then dip in egg mixture followed by corn flake mixture. Ensure both sides are well coated and pat with fingers to ensure that the coating stays on.
8.	Place fish in air fryer basket. Arrange them in a single layer, do not stack.
9.	Cook for 8-10 minutes until it is lightly browned. Flip over halfway through your cooking
10.	Return fries to basket and heat slightly. Can be served with tarter sauce if desired.

Time: 15 minutes | Amount: 8 servings

Ingredients:

- 8 fish fillets (28 oz/ 800g)
- Olive oil (1 tbsp)
- Bread crumbs (1 cup)
- Paparika
- Chili powder
- Garlic powder and Black pepper (1/4 tsp each)
- Onion powder ((1/4 tsp)
- Salt (1/2 tsp)

How to prepare:

1.	Defrost fillets if frozen. Drizzle with oil till its well coated
2.	Mix breadcrumbs with paprika in a shallow bowl. Add chilli pepper, garlic powder, salt, black pepper & onion powder to the mix
3.	Coat each of your fish fillets with the breadcrumb mixture
4.	Transfer to and cook in air fryer at 200C/390F for about 15 minutes. Flip over after about 8 minutes the continue cooking.

Time: 25 minutes | Amount:8 servings

Ingredients:

- Cod fillet (about 1.5 lb/0.7kg)
- Salt
- Pepper
- Flour (1/2 cup)
- 1 egg+ 1 tbsp of water
- Crumbs (cracker or cornflake crumbs)-1/2 cup
- Vegetable oil (1 tbsp)
- For the Sauce

- low fat Mayonnaise (1/2 cup)
- Honey (1 tsp)
- Finely minced lemon zest and juice (form half lemon)
- Worcestershire sauce (1/2 teaspoon)
- Black pepper
- sweet pickle relish(1 tbsp)

How to prepare:

1.	Crush the crackers (or corn flakes) bread crumbs into finer bits using a food processor
2.	Season cod chunks with some pepper and salt and dredge into flour
3.	Next, dip cod chunks into egg wash then inot cracker crumbs. Ensure it is completely coated on every side.
4.	Preheat air fryer to 180oC/360oF
5.	Arrange as many of the cod as possible into the basket on a single row without stacking. You can use the rack to cook as well
6.	Cook for about 15 minutes. Remove fish from the basket. To be served with garden salad, french fries or Lemon Tarter sauce
7.	To prepare sauce, blend all listed ingredients. Leave in refrigerator while the cod cooks.

Time: 35 minutes | Amount:6 servings

Ingredients:

- Sour cream (1 tablespoon)
- Mayonnaise (1 tbsp)
- 1 Finely chopped garlic clove
- Lime juice (1 teaspoon)
- Salt (1/4 teaspoon)
- Shredded green cabbage (1 1/2 c)
- Taco seasoning mix (2 tbsp)
- 1/4 cup red onion (thinly sliced)
- 1 egg
- Plain Panko crispy breadcrumbs (1/2 cup)
- Water (1 tbsp)
- White fish fillets (one lb/0.45 kg) cut into strips 1 inch each
- Mini flour tortilla taco bowls (1 package of 12 bowls)
- Sliced avocado,
- Cilantro leaves (freshly chopped)
- Lime wedges
- Radishes (thinly sliced)

How to prepare:

1.	Mix sour cream, garlic, mayonnaise, lime juice and salt in a medium-sized bowl bowl. Add red onions and cabbage to the mix and toss to coat. Cover mixture and refrigerate. Keep until it is time to serve
2.	Cut parchment paper (8-inches round) and place at the bottom of air fryer basket
3.	Pour taco seasoning mix into a shallow bowl. In another shallow dish, beat egg with some water. In a third blow pour the bread crumb. Coat the fish starting with the taco seasoning mix then dip into egg mixture and finally the bread crumb mixture.
4.	Place coated fish on parchment at the bottom of air fryer basket. Cook for 8 minutes at air fryer temperature of 350°F or180°C. Turn the fish half-way through cooking. Continue to cook until fish begins to flake.
5.	Cut fish into bit fishes
6.	Scoop cabbage mixture into taco bowl. Top this with fish, avocado, cilantro and radishes. Can be served with lime wedges.

Time: 10 minutes | Amount: 2 to 4 servings

Ingredients:

♦ Small fish (e.g. kembung)

♦ For marinade:

♦ Sea salt

♦ Turmeric powder

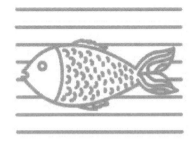

How to prepare:

1.	Cut and remove fish intestines. Clean then pat dry
2.	Marinate in salt and turmeric mixture for about 30 minutes
3.	Arrange marinated fish in air fryer basket. Air fry at about 360 degrees F or 180 degrees C. for the first 5 minutes. Turn up the heat to about 400 degrees F for 8 more minutes
4.	Remove from air fryer and serve hot with chili sauce

Time: 30 minutes | Amount:4 servings

Ingredients:

- Peeled and seeded butternut squash (1 small) cut into small 1 inch pieces
- Olive oil (4 tbsp)
- Paula Deen's House Seasoning (1tsp)
- Lemon juice (2 tbsp)
- Shallot (1 small) minced
- Salt (1/4 tsp)
- Arugula (6 oz/170g)
- Granny smith apple (1 small) cored and sliced
- Parmesan cheese (1/2 cup) grated
- Sliced almonds (1/2 cups)

How to prepare:

1.	Mix squash, olive oil, cayenne pepper and House seasoning in a large bowl.
2.	Place squash in your air fryer and cook for about 15 minutes at 400 degrees F/ 205 degrees C. shake occasionally. Set aside when done
3.	Whisk lemon juice, salt, shallot and olive oil in another large bowl. Toss together with Arugula until it is well coated. Divide coated arugula between 4 plates then top with squash and some apple slices.
4.	Serve chilled, sprinkled with Parmesan cheese & sliced almond

Time: 40 minutes | Amount: 4 servings

Ingredients:

- ◆ Sweet potato (1 medium)
- ◆ Capsicum (yellow and red)
- ◆ Onions (1 red)
- ◆ Small chat potatoes (4)
- ◆ Cherry tomatoes (250g/8oz)
- ◆ Mixed salad leaves (300g/10oz bag)
- ◆ Cumin (1 tsp)
- ◆ Lemon juice (from 2 lemons)
- ◆ Chopped capers (2 tbsp)
- ◆ Fresh parsley
- ◆ Avocado
- ◆ Olive oil (1 tbsp)
- ◆ Salt and pepper (added to taste)
- ◆ Chickpeas (1 tin)
- ◆ Mustard powder (1 tsp)

How to prepare:

1.	Chop all vegetables roughly. Season with salt and pepper lightly. Throw all into air fryer basket. Cook at 390oF/200oC for 25 minutes. Shake basket halfway through the cooking to ensure it is cooked evenly. Remove veggies and place in fridge overnight
2.	Toss vegetable mixture in some fresh rocket. Prepare dressing by mashing avocado then mixing with oil, chopped parsley, cumin, caper and lemon juice.
3.	Toss salad and serve

Time: 25 minutes | Amount:4 servings

Ingredients:

- Broccoli (1lbs/0.45kg)
- Olive oil (3 tbsp)
- Salt
- Pepper
- Garlic (4 crushed cloves)
- Lemon and flaky salt (as finish)-optional

How to prepare:

1.	Toss the broccoli along with olive oil, garlic cloves. Add pepper & salt to taste.
2.	After tossing put in air fryer and cook at 400oF/205oC for 10 minutes. Shake the basket after 10 minutes then return to fryer and cook for an additional 10 minute.
3.	Check and shake occasionally.
4.	Remove from heat once charred optimally

Time: 20 minutes | Amount: 4 servings

Ingredients:

- Cauliflower (1 small head) cut into small florets
- Drizzle of olive oil
- Beets (3 small) cut into small wedges (about 1/4 inch)
- Salt (to taste)

How to prepare:

1.	Preheat air fryer to 360oF/182oC.
2.	Toss cauliflower in a bowl along with some olive oil & salt
3.	In another bowl, toss beets with olive oil and pepper
4.	Arrange beets in air fryer basket (keep in a single layer). Cook for 12-13 minutes. Turn once, halfway through the cooking. Remove when done
5.	Arrange cauliflower mixture in the fry basket of your air fryer. Cook for 8 minutes stirring only during cooking. Work in batches if required

Time: 27 minutes | Amount: 4 servings

Ingredients:

- Eggs (6 large)
- Corns (3 ears) cut in smaller pieces
- Vegetable or canola oil (2 tsp)
- Salt & pepper (added to taste)
- Red onion (1/4 cup) sliced
- Julienned carrots, green pepper and red bell pepper (1/2 c each)

For dressing:

- Mayonnaise (1 cup)
- Dijon mustard (one tbsp)(can use Yellow too)
- Maple syrup (1 tsp) (or honey)
- Pepper and salt (added to taste)

How to prepare:

1.	Add eggs to a trivet placed in your air fryer basket
2.	Air fry egg for 20 minutes at 250oF/121oC. Submerge eggs in ice bath when time elapses to discontinue cooking.
3.	Peel eggs and dice into chunks
4.	Cut corn cobs into smaller pieces. Coat these in vegetable oil. Sprinkle with pepper & salt to taste. Air fry this at 400oF/205oC. Cook for about 10 minutes, flipping once halfway through the cooking
5.	When corn is done, carefully separate kernels from cob using a knife.
6.	In a side bowl, mix dressing ingredients and whisk. Add dressing to your corn and egg salad then toss to mix thoroughly.
7.	Cove r and leave to chill for about an hour
8.	Keep refrigerated or serve as side to grilled meat or any meal of your choice .

Time: 20 minutes | Amount:4 servings

Ingredients:

- Panko breadcrumbs (1/2 cups)
- Salt (1/2 tsp)
- 1 Avocado (Haas) peeled sliced and pitted
- Aquafuba (from 1 ounce can) garbanzo beans or white beans

How to prepare:

1.	Toss panko breadcrumbs and salt together in a shallow bowl. In another bowl, add aquafuba
2.	Dredge avocado slices in aquafaba then in panko to get a nice and even coating
3.	Arrange avocado slices in a single layer in the air fryer basket. Ensure that there is no overlapping. Air fryer at 390oF/195oC for 10 minutes. (do not preheat air fryer). check and shake well after 5 minutes.

Time: 10 minutes | Amount: 2 servings

Ingredients:

- Olive oil (2 tbsp)
- Kale (loosely packed)- 4 cups (stemmed)
- Vegan ranch seasoning (2 tsp)
- Nutritional yeast flakes (1 tbsp)
- Salt (1/4 tsp)

How to prepare:

1.	In a medium bowl, toss kale pieces, oil, ranch seasoning and yeast
2.	Dump coated kale into air fryer basket
3.	Cook for 4 to 5 minutes at about 370oF/185oC (do not preheat the fryer). Shake basket after 2 minutes to ensure even cooking
4.	To be served immediately.

Time: 25 minutes | Amount:4 servings

Ingredients:

- Dry ingredients
- All-purpose flour (1/2 c)
- Baking soda (1/8 tsp)
- Salt (1/8 tsp)

Wet Ingredients

- Brown sugar and Organic sugar (1 tbsp each)

- Vegan butter (1 tbsp) softened but not melted
- Vanilla extract (1/4 tsp)
- Aquafaba (2 tbsp)
- Vegan chocolate chips (1/4 cup)

How to prepare:

1.	Combine all dry ingredients in a bowl.
2.	In another bowl, cream vegan butter, brown and organic sugars with vanilla extract. Also add the aquafaba and beat thoroughly
3.	Add all wet ingredients to dry ingredients (also add vegan chocolate chips). Mix until it all forms a a ball of sticky dough. Use your hands if necessary
4.	Cover most of your air fryer basket using parchment paper. Leave an inch of space on all sides for easy air flow.
5.	Place the dough ball on parchment paper then place another paper over it. Press the cookie dough into a big round cookie (about 1/4 inches thick). make the cookie as even as possible to ensure uniform cooking. Remove the top parchment paper.
6.	Cook in air fryer at 350oF/175oF for 10 minutes. Remove basket from fryer, leave for 10 minutes to cool before transferring cookie to a plate.

Time: 20 minutes | Amount: 6 servings

Ingredients:

- Trimmed fresh green beans (24 oz./680g)
- Button mushrooms (sliced) 2 cups
- lemon juice (fresh- from 1 lemon)
- Garlic powder (1 tbsp)
- Ground sage (3/4 tsp)
- Salt (3/4 tsp)
- Onion powder (1 tsp)
- Black paper (3/4 tsp)
- Spray oil
- French fried onion (1/3 cups) for garnish (not mandatory)

How to prepare:

1.	Toss green beans, mushrooms, garlic powder, salt, pepper and lemon juice in a bowl.
2.	Transfer mixture to air fryer basket. Spray to coat.
3.	Cook at 400oF/205oC for 10-12 minutes. Check and shake every 2 or 3 minutes
4.	Can be served with french fried onions

Time: 42 minutes | Amount: 15 -20 yields

Ingredients:

For Cheese

- ◆ Raw cashews (1/2 cup) preboiled for 10 minutes)
- ◆ Nutritional Yeast (3 tbsp)
- ◆ Tapioca Starch (3 tbsp + 2 tsp)
- ◆ Apple cider vinegar (1 tsp)
- ◆ Water (11/4 cup)

For samboosa

- ◆ Olive oil (1 tbsp)
- ◆ Water (1/2 cup)

How to prepare:

1.	Mix all the ingredients for the cheese using a blender until they are smooth
2.	Pour this mixture into a saucepan and heat over medium heat. Stir continually as you cook using a spatula or wooden spoon. Do this for 5 minutes or until it is all firmed up
3.	Leave this to cool in a glass container in the refrigerator for 30 minutes or more
4.	Place samosa sheet vertically on a plate or cutting board. Add a light wash of water with a pastry brush to help the edges stick together (especially if the sheets are dry)
5.	Add about 2 tsp of cheese mixture to far right corner of sheet. Fold the pastry sheet from the bottom right point to form a triangle shape over filling. Take the top right point of this triangle and fold again horizontally this time. Alternate these steps unitl you have a parcel with a triangular shape. Seal down this final flap
6.	Do this until you use up all samosa sheets.
7.	Brush each of these wraps with olive oil on both side. Place 4 to 6 parcels in air-fryer depending on the size of your unit and cook at 200oC/390oF for 6 to 10 minutes or until crisp and lightly browned

Time: 15 minutes | Amount: 4 servings

Ingredients:

♦ Stale cinnamon raisin bagels

♦ Melted butter

♦ Cinnamon sugar

How to prepare:

1.	Cut the stale cinnamon raisin bagel into thin rounds
2.	Brush with the melted butter then sprinkle with some sugar
3.	Cook in preheated air fryer at 360oF/180oC for about 5 minutes
4.	Flip then brush with some butter then add cinnamon sugar
5.	Bake again for 5 additional minutes
6.	Pour source in the bowl of pasta and stir to combine. Serve immediately. Can be kept chilled and covered for up to 4 days. Gently reheat and add some water to loosen the sauce.

Time: 20 minutes | Amount:6 cups

Ingredients:

- ◆ Dried corn kernels (3 tbsp)
- ◆ Avocado oil
- ◆ Sea salt
- ◆ Pepper (to taste)
- ◆ Garnish
- ◆ 2 tbsp
- ◆ Dried chives

How to prepare:

1.	Set air fryer to 390oF/199oC
2.	Add kernels to fryer basket then spray lightly. You can line the air fryer tray with an aluminium foil to hold corns from flying around inside fryer as they pop.
3.	Cook for 15 minutes but check every 3-5 minutes to ensure that the kernels don't burn Continue to monitor until popping sound stops.
4.	Remove basket and dump content in a large bowl. Spray lightly with avocado or coconut oil. Dust with garnish
5.	Serve warm

Time: 55 minutes | Amount: 4 servings

Ingredients:

- 1 tofu (block firm) pressed then cut into small 1inch cubes
- Soy sauce (2 tbsp)
- Seasoned rice vinegar (1 tsp)
- Sesame oil (2 tsp)
- Potato or corn starch (1tbsp)

How to prepare:

1.	Toss tofu, vinegar, soy sauce and oil together in a shallow bowl. Set this aside and leave to marinate for 15 to 30 minutes
2.	Toss marinated tofu with corn starch (or potato starch) then pour into air fryer basket.
3.	Cook for 20 minutes at 370oF/180oC. Shake after 10 minutes to ensure uniform cooking

Time: 15minutes | Amount: 4 to 6 servings

Ingredients:

- 2 sweet potatoes (medium sized) thinly sliced
- Olive oil (1/4 cup)
- Ground cinnamon (1 tsp)
- Salt
- Pepper

How to prepare:

1.	With a food processor or mandolin, cut sweet potatoes into thin slices
2.	Soak slices in water for 30 minutes
3.	Drain then pat dry thoroughly until it is completely dry
4.	Toss slices together with olive oil, cinnammon, salt and pepper
5.	Air fry in greased air fryer basket at 390oF/190oC for 20 minutes. Shake basket every 7 minutes to ensure even cooking. Cook until crisp
6.	To be served hot with ketchup

Time: 20 minutes | Amount:3 servings

Ingredients:

♦   Chicken breasts (12 oz/320g)

♦   Egg white (from one egg)

♦   Flour (1/8 cup)

♦   Panko bread crumbs (35g/1.2oz)

♦   Salt

♦   Pepper

How to prepare:

1.	Trim chicken breast to remove excess fat. Cut into tenders
2.	Add salt and pepper to season. Ensure both sides are properly seasoned
3.	Dip tenders into flour, then dip in the bowl of egg white. Finally dip in panko breadcrumbs to coat
4.	Load tenders into air fryer basket. Cook at 350oF/175oC
5.	Cook for about 10 minutes or until properly cooked through

Time: 40 minutes | Amount: 4 servings

Ingredients:

- 1 egg plant (large about 1.5 lbs/0.7kg)
- Breadcrumbs (1/2 cup)
- Parmesan cheese (3 tbsp) (finely grated)
- Salt (added to taste)
- Italian seasoning (1 tsp)
- Flour (whole wheat) 3 tbsp
- 1 egg
- Water (1 tbsp)
- Cooking spray
- Marinara sauce (1 cup)
- Mozzarella cheese (grated) 1/4 cup
- Parsley or basil (to garnish)

How to prepare:

1.	Cut the eggplant into smaller slices (about 1/2 inches per slice). rub salt on both side of each slice and leave for about 10 to 15 minutes.
2.	Mix egg, water and flour in a bowl to prepare batter
3.	In a medium plate, mix bread crumbs and Parmesan cheese. Add Italian seasoning mix and some salt.
4.	Apply batter to each slice of eggplant and spread evenly. Dip battered slices into the breadcrumb mix to coat.
5.	Place coated slices on a clean and lat plate and spray with cooking oil.
6.	Preheat air fryer to about 360oF/180oC. Cook eggplant slices on the air fryer wire mesh for about 8 minutes.
7.	Top slices with 1 tbsp of marinara sauce then spread mozzarella cheese on it. Cook for 2 additional minutes or until cheese melts.
8.	To be served warm with your favorite pasta.

Time: 10 minutes | Amount: 4 servings

Ingredients:

- 2 limes (juiced)
- 1 orange (medium) peeled and seeded
- Cilantro (1 cup)
- Vegetable oil (2 tbsp)
- White vinegar (2 tbsp)
- Ancho Chile powder (2 tsp)
- Splenda (1tsp) or sugar (2 tsp)
- Salt (1 tsp)
- Cummin seeds (1 tsp)
- Coriander seeds (1 tsp)
- Skirt steak (1. 5 lbs/0.7kg)

How to prepare:

1.	Place all your ingredients except skirt steak in a blender. Blend till sauce reaches a smooth consistency.
2.	Cut steak into four smaller pieces and place in a zip-top bag
3.	Pour blended blended over steak & leave to marinate for 30 minutes. You can refrigerate overnight if desired.
4.	Set air fryer to about 400oF/205oC. Place steaks into air fryer basket. Do not stack. Cook in small batches to avoid stacking
5.	Cook for 8 minutes. Ensure that you do not overcook the steak or the meat will toughen.
6.	Leave to rest for about 10 minutes before serving. To serve, cut steak against the grain.

Time: 45 minutes | Amount: 4 servings

Ingredients:

- Bulk pork sausage (1lb/0.45kg)
- Finely chopped chives (1 tbsp)
- Finely-chopped parsley (2 tbsp)
- Grated nutmeg (1/8 tsp)
- Salt (1/8 tsp)
- Ground black pepper (1/8 teaspoons)
- 4 eggs (hard cooked and peeled)
- shredded Parmesan cheese (1 cup)
- coarse-ground mustard (2 tsp)

How to prepare:

1.	Gently mix sausage, chives, mustard, parsely, salt, black pepper and nutmeg in a large bowl until it is well combined. Shape mixture into 4 patties of similar size
2.	Place one egg on each sausage party then shape the patty around the egg. Dip each in shredded Parmesan cheese until it is completely covered. Ensure that the cheese shreds are well-pressed into the meat.
3.	Arrange in the air fryer. Spray lightly with cooking spray or vegetable oil. Set your fryer to about 400ºF/ 205ºC.cook for 15 minutes. Turn eggs halfway through cooking and spray again.
4.	Can be served with the coarse ground mustard.

Time: 35 minutes | Amount: 2 servings

Ingredients:

- Bourbon (1 tbsp)
- Brown sugar (2 tbsp)
- Maple bacon (cut in half) 3 strips
- Ground beef (80% lean)
- Minced onion (1 tbsp)
- BBQ sauce (2 tbsp)
- Salt (1 tsp)
- Black pepper (freshly ground)
- Colby jack cheese (2 slices)
- 2 Kaiser rolls
- Lettuce and tomatoes (for servings)

For Zesty burger sauce:

- BBQ sauce (2 tbsp)
- Mayonnaise (2 tbsp)
- Ground Paprika (1/4 tsp)
- Ground black pepper

How to prepare:

1.	Preheat air fryer to about 390ºF/200oC. Add little water to airfryer base to prevent smoking.
2.	In a small bowl, combine bourbon and brown sugar. Coat bacon strips with this mixture.
3.	Place strips in air fryer and cook for 4 minutes. Flip bacon over, brush with more of this brown sugar mixture and air fry for 4 more minutes until it becomes crispy.
4.	Make burger patties while bacon is cooking by mixing ground beef, onion, BBQ sauce, pepper and salt. Mix thoroughly then shape into 2 patties.
5.	Transfer patties to air fryer and cook at 370ºF/180oC for 15 to 20 minutes. Flip over halfway through the cooking.
6.	Prepare burger sauce by combining ingredient in a bowl
7.	Top each burger patty with a slice of colby jack cheese. Return to air fryer for about a minute (for the cheese to melt)
8.	Spread sauce inside Kaiser roll, place burgers on the roll, top with bourbon bacon, lettuce and tomato to serve.

Time: 25 minutes | Amount: 4 servings

Ingredients:

For Bulgogi Burgers

◆ Ground beef (1 lb/0.48g) (use lean beef)

◆ Gochujang (2 tbsp)

◆ Dark soy sauce (1 tablespoon)

◆ Minced garlic and ginger (2 tsp each)

◆ Sugar (2 tsp)

◆ Sesame oil (1 tablespoon)

◆ Green onions (1/4 cup)

◆ Salt (1/2 tsp)

For Gochujang Mayonaisse

◆ Mayonnaise (1/4 c)

◆ Gochujang (1 tsp)

◆ Sesame Oil (1 tsp)

◆ Chopped Scallions (1/4 c)

◆ Sesame seeds (2 tsp)

◆ 4 hamburger buns (for serving)

How to prepare:

1.	Mix ground beef, soy sauce, gochujang, garlic, ginger, sesame seed, oil, salt and chopped onions in a bowl. Leave this to rest for 30 minutes. (can be left for up to 24 hours in a refridgerator)
2.	Divide meat into four portions. From round patties with each portion. Form a slight depression in the middle of each piece to prevent it from puffing into a dome-shape
3.	Set air fryer to 360oF/180oC. Preheat for about 10 minutes then place patties in the air fryer basket in a single later. Cook until the internal temperature of the meat reaches about 160oF/ 70oC then remove to serving plate
4.	Serve patties with hamburger bun and gochujang mayonnaise.
5.	Cook for 8 minutes. Ensure that you do not overcook the steak or the meat will toughen.
6.	Leave to rest for about 10 minutes before serving. To serve, cut steak against the grain.

Time: 10 minutes | Amount: 4 servings

Ingredients:

- Ribeye steak (1 lb/0.48kg)
- Brown sugar (1 tsp)
- Coarse sea salt (1 1/2 tsp)
- Ground coffee (1/2 tsp)
- Onion powder & garlic (1/4 tsp each)
- Black pepper (1/2 tsp)
- Chilli powder (1/4 tsp)
- Paprika (1/4 tsp)
- Chipotle powder (1/4 tsp)
- Coriander (1/8 tsp)
- Cocoa powder (1/8 tsp)

How to prepare:

1.	Whisk all spices in bowl. ensure that brown sugar are well broken
2.	Sprinkle spice mix into a large plate, lay steak on top of spices then season generously with more of it. Rub the spices into the meat using your fingers. Ensure that both sides are properly seasoned
3.	Set aside steak for 20 minutes or more till it cools to room temperature. l
4.	Preheat air fryer for 3 minutes on 390oF/200oC. Spray basket with cooking spray or oil
5.	Cook steak for at least 9 minutes without flipping or opening air dryer. Remove from air dryer and leave for 5 minutes before you slice and serve.
6.	Leave to rest for about 10 minutes before serving. To serve, cut steak against the grain.

Time: 25 minutes | Amount: 2 servings

Ingredients:

- Fresh asperagus spears (10)
- Vegetable oil
- 1 large egg
- Parmesan cheese (1/3 cup)
- Heavy whipping cream (1 tbsp)
- Paprika (1/2 tsp)
- Almond flour (1/3 cup)
- Salt (1/2 tsp)

For Dip:

- Mayonnaise (1/4 cup)
- Dijon mustard (1 teaspoon)
- Cayanne (1/4 teaspoon)
- Black pepper (1/4 tsp)

How to prepare:

1.	Mix all dip ingredients in a bowl. Set aside, refrigerated until you are need to use.
2.	Cut off the tough woody ends of the asparagus spears until you are left with about 6 inches. Rinse them and pat to dry
3.	Beat egg and heavy cream together in bowl. Pour mixture into shallow plate. '
4.	In a different shallow plate, mix all breading ingredients until they are well mixed.
5.	coat each asperagus spear in egg wash, transfer to the breading and coat again until it is well coated on all side. Transfer coated asparagus to perchment paper. Do this for each asperagus spear
6.	Fry breaded asparagus in air fryer for about 3 to 5 minutes until golden. Remove & drain using paper towels.
7.	Serve hot along with the prepared dip

Time: 26 minutes | Amount: 4 servings

Ingredients:

- Onion (1 sliced)
- Flour (1 1/4 cups)
- Baking powder (1 tsp)n
- 1 egg (beaten)
- Milk (49tsp)
- Bread crumb seasoning (3/4 cup + 1 tsp)

How to prepare:

1.	Preheat air fryer to 370oF/180oC. Spray air fryer basket with non-stick oil
2.	Mix flour, seasoning and baking powder in a mixing bowl. Add the eggs, milk (or beer). Transfer this mixture to a shallow bowl
3.	In a shallow bowl, place bread crumbs. Using a fork, take onion slice and cover with the flour mixture then dip this into breadcrumbs bowl.
4.	Place this into the air fryer basket. Repeat for all onion slices.
5.	Air fry for 8 minutes. Flip over then Fry for another 8 minutes until done.
6.	Fry breaded asparagus in air fryer for about 3 to 5 minutes until golden. Remove & drain using paper towels.
7.	Serve hot along with the prepared dip

Time: 8 minutes | Amount: 2 servings

Ingredients:

- Beef flak steak (sliced into thin long strips) 1 lb/0.48kg
- Oil (2 tbsp)
- Fish sauce (1 tbsp)
- Soy sauce (1 tbsp)
- Minced ginger (1 tbsp)
- Minced garlic (1 tbsp)
- Sugar (1 tbsp)
- Sriracha Sauce (1 tsp)
- Ground coriander (1 tsp)
- Chopped cilantro (1/2 cup)
- Roasted peanuts (chopped) 1/2 cup

How to prepare:

1.	In a large bowl or zip-lock bag, place beef strips. Add oil, fish and soy sauce, garlic, ginger, sriracha, sugar, coriander, cilantro to the beef. Mix well and marinate for about 30 minutes. (can be kept refigerated for up to 24 hours)
2.	Place beef strips in air fryer basket. lay them side by side to avoid overlap
3.	Set fryer to about 400F/205C and cook beef for about 8 minutes. Flip when it is halfway cooked.
4.	Remove meat. Place in serving plate and Top with remaining cilantro and roasted peanuts
5.	Serve with Peanut sauce

Time: 21 minutes | Amount: 4 servings

Ingredients:

- Pork rinds- crushed (1/2 cup)
- Finely grated Parmesan cheese (3 tbsp)
- Dill pickles (16 slices)
- Almond flour (1/2 cup)
- Egg (1 large)
- Cooking spray

How to prepare:

1.	In a medium bowl, mix Parmesan cheese and pork rinds. In another bowl, add whisked egg. Put almond flour in a third bowl
2.	Dredge each pickle in almond flour, then egg and finally in the bowl of pork rind mixture
3.	Place pickle in greased air fryer forming a single layer of breaded pickles
4.	Spray with olive oik
5.	Cook in fryer for 6 minutes at 370oF/180oC

Time: 25 minutes | Amount: 5 servings

Ingredients:

- 5 jalapenos (medium)
- Goat cheese (4 oz/113g)
- Salt (to taste)

For Salsa:

- Onion
- Cilantro
- Crushed red pepper
- Garlic
- Chilli powder

How to prepare:

1.	De-seed jalapanos and halve
2.	Add the salsa blend and salt to goat cheese. Mix thoroughly using a fork
3.	Spoon mixture into jalapeno halves. Place in a air fryer basket
4.	Cook at 350 degrees F/180 degrees C for about 8 minutes until jalapenos are soft or crispy

Time: 15 minutes | Amount: 4 strips

Ingredients:

- Bacon (4 strips)
- Hot sauce(1/4 cup)
- Crushed pork rinds (1/2 cup)

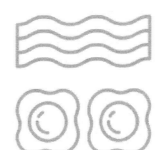

How to prepare:

1.	Cut the bacon slices into even pieces then place them in a large bowl
2.	To this bowl, add hot sauce. Ensure that both sides of the bacon are covered with the sauce
3.	Dip the bacon pieces into the crushed pork rides to coat it completely
4.	Cook in air fryer at 350oF/170oC for about 10 minutes. Check after about 8 minutes to make sure that it is not burning.

Time: 25 minutes | Amount: 2 servings

Ingredients:

- Frozen spinach- thawad (10 oz/280g package)
- Chopped onions (1/2 cup)
- Minced garlic (2 tsp)
- Ground nutmeg (1/2 tsp)
- Cream cheese (4 oz/118g) diced
- Ground black pepper (1 tsp)
- Salt (1 tsp)
- Parmesan cheese (1/4 cup)

How to prepare:

1.	Grease and set aside a 6-inch pan
2.	Combine spinach, garlic, onion, cream cheese, pepper, nutmeg & salt in a bowl. Pour this mixture into prepared greased pan
3.	Place pan in air dryer at 350ºF/175ºC for about 10 minutes.
4.	Open air fryer and stir the spinach to ensure that it is well mixed with the cream cheese
5.	Add parmesan cheese, increase air fryer heat to 400ºF/204ºC and leave for 5 minutes or till the cheese is melted.

Time: 21 minutes | Amount: 3 servings

Ingredients:

- Shrimp (cleaned and peeled) 1 lb/0.48kg
- Coconut flour (3/4 c
- Onion and garlic powder (1 tsp each)
- 2 lightly beaten eggs
- Pork rind crumbs (1/2 cup)
- Unsweetened shredded coconut flakes (1/2 cup)
- Fresh pepper
- Kosher salt
- Avocado/grape seed oil

How to prepare:

1.	Add coconut flour, garlic, onion powder, salt, some pepper to shallow dish. Mix thoroughly
2.	To a small dish, add eggs and whisk lightly
3.	To a zip-top bag, add pork rinds. Bash them to small breadcrumbs using a rolling pin. Add this to a small dish along with coconut flakes, 1/4 tsp salt and some pepper then mix well.
4.	Season shrimp on both sides with salt then dredge in the coconut flour mixture. Shake off any excess then dredge in eggs. Finally dredge in the pro rind and coconut flakes until shrimp is well coated.
5.	Move shrimp to wire rack and repeat process for the remaining shrimps.
6.	Spray air fryer basket with cooking oil and fry shrimps at 390oF/200oC for about 8 minutes. Flip shrimp halfway through the cooking

Time: 20 minutes | Amount: 4 servings

Ingredients:

- Cod or any other White fish (1 lb/0.48kg)
- Mayonnaise (1/4 cup)
- Dijon Mustard (2 tbsp)
- Water (2 tbsp)
- Pork rind panko (11/2 cups)
- Cajun seasoning (3/4 tsp)
- Pepper and salt (added to taste)

How to prepare:

1.	Spray air fryer rack with cooking spray
2.	Pat fish dry then cut into sticks (each stick should be about 1 inch by 2 inches wide)
3.	In a shallow bowl, combine the mayo and mustard with water. In another bowl whisk pork rinds and the cajun seasoning then add some salt and pepper to taste (note: pork rinds and cajun seasoning may have some salt in them already)
4.	Dip fish in mayo mixture to coat. Tap off excess and dip in pork rind mixture until it is well coated. Repeat this process for all the fish pieces.
5.	Set air fryer to 400oF/205oC and bake fish for 5 minutes. Flip fish sticks and bake for five more minutes. To be served immediately.

Time: 25 minutes | Amount: 4 servings

Ingredients:

- Chicken breast (boneless and skinless) 1 lb/0.48kg
- Sea salt
- Sesame oil (1 tsp)
- Coconut flour (1/4 c)
- Ground ginger (1 tsp)
- Egg whites (from 4 eggs)
- Toasted sesame seeds (6 tbsp)

- Cooking spray

For the dip:

- Natural almond butter (2 tbsp)
- Coconut aminos (4 tsp)
- Water (1 tbsp)
- Rice vinegar (2 tsp)
- Ground ginger (1/2 tsp)
- Monkfruit (1/2 tsp) optional

How to prepare:

1.	Preheat air fryer to 400oF/205oC for about 10 minutes
2.	while preheating air fryer, cut chicken breasts (about an inch per piece of nugget) dry then place them in a bowl. Toss with sesame oil and salt to coat
3.	In a large ziploc bag place coconut flour along with ground ginger and shake to mix. Add chicken pieces then shake until fully coated
4.	in a large bowl, place egg white and add chicken. Toss until is it fully coated
5.	In a large ziploc bag, place sesame seeds, and add nuggets to the bag. Shake until is it well coated.
6.	Spray air fryer basket with some cooing spray. Place nuggets in the basket and spray with cooking spray again.
7.	Cook in fryer for 6 minutes flip nuggets and spray then cook for 6 more minutes or until nuggets are crispy inside.
8.	To prepare dip, whisk all ingredients in a bowl. Mix well until smooth.

Time: 15 minutes | Amount: 24 tots

Ingredients:

- Cauliflower (2 cups)
- Garlic powder (1/2 tsp)
- Rotisserie seasoned Chicken Breast (8 oz/226g) chopped
- Parmesan cheese (3/4 c)
- 1 egg

For Breading

- Parmesan cheese (4 tbsp)
- Almond flour (6 tbsp)

How to prepare:

1.	Using a food processor, chop cauliflower into pearls
2.	In a large bowl, combine the cauliflower with chopped chicken, garlic powder, Parmesan cheese, and buffalo sauce. Mix well until fully combined then roll into balls about 1 tsp in size
3.	In a separate bowl prepare breading by mixing 4 tbps of Parmesan cheese and 6 tbsp of almond flour
4.	Roll each chicken ball in coating to form tarter tot shapes. Fry in air fryer for about 5 minutes flipping occasionally to ensure it cooks uniformly. Remove when tots are golden brown
5.	Spread open the wedges and add the taco meat into the tomatoes. Add cheese, sour cream and lettuce to top.

Time: 20 minutes | Amount: 11 slices

Ingredients:

♦ 11 bacon slices

How to prepare:

1.	Divide bacon into two portion, place first half in air fryer
2.	Set the temperature to 400oF/205oC and cook for 10 minutes (less for thinner slices)
3.	Check halfway through and turn over if there is need for it. Check to see if bacon is done.
4.	Repeat the process for the other half.

Time: 20 minutes | Amount: 8 servings

Ingredients:

- Ground beef with 80/20 fat (1 lb/0.48kg)n
- 2 eggs (lightly beaten)
- Finely chopped onions (1/4 cup)
- Extra fine almond flour (1/2 cup)
- Coconut flour (1/4 cup)
- Minced garlic (1 clove)
- Italian Seasoning (1 tsp)
- Ketchup (1/4 cup)
- Sea salt (1/2 tsp)
- Worcestershire Sauce (1 tbsp)
- Black pepper (1/2 tsp)
- Dried Terragon (1/2 tsp)

How to prepare:

1.	Mix all ingredients in a large bowl. Make patties with this, each should be about 2 inches in diameter with a thickness of about 1 inch. Ensure their sizes are similar to ensure uniform cooking
2.	Refrigerate patties for 10 minutes. This ensures that all the wet ingredient are absorbed by the flour making the patties firm.
3.	Preheat fryer to 360°F/180°C
4.	Place patties in air fryer basket. Cook for10 minutes. Check halfway through cooking. You can cook sliders in batches for uniform cooking
5.	Can be served with paleo breads, lettuce wraps or biscuits

Time:50 minutes | Amount: 4 servings

Ingredients:

- Olive oil (extra-virgin)
- Chopped onions (1 cup)
- Garlic (1 clove)-minced
- Ground beef (1 lb/0.45kg)
- Kosher salt
- Black pepper
- Chopped cilantro (2 tbsp)
- Ground cumin (1/2 tsp)
- Smoked paprika (1/2 tsp)

- Bell peppers (3 peppers) halved and seeded
- Shredded cheddar (1 cup)
- Monterey jack (1 cup)-shredded
- Shredded lettuce
- Pico de gallo, Hot sauce and lime wedges (for serving)

How to prepare:

1.	Heat olive oil over medium heat in a skillet
2.	Add onions and leave to cook for about 4 minutes until it is tender. Add garlic and cook for 1 additional minute. To this, add ground beef then cook for 5 minutes or until the color is no longer pink.
3.	Add spices to this and also season with salt and pepper
4.	Drizzle bell peppers with olive oil & season with salt and pepper. Spoon some of the cooked beef mixture onto the bell peppers. Top these with cheese.
5.	Place these in a preheated air fryer. Cook for 30 minutes or until peppers become crisp and tender.
6.	Serve topped with lettuce or with pico de gello, hot sauce and lime wedges.

The opinions and ideas of the author contained in this publication are designed to educate the reader in an informative and helpful manner. While we accept that the instructions will not suit every reader, it is only to be expected that the recipes might not gel with everyone. Use the book responsibly and at your own risk. This work with all its contents, does not guarantee correctness, completion, quality or correctness of the provided information. Always check with your medical practitioner should you be unsure whether to follow a low carb eating plan. Misinformation or misprints cannot be completely eliminated. Human error is real!

Printed in Great Britain
by Amazon